Writings of William Law

Upper Room Spiritual Classics®

Selected, edited, and introduced by
KEITH BEASLEY-TOPLIFFE

UPPER ROOM BOOKS®
NASHVILLE

WRITINGS OF WILLIAM LAW

Previously published as *Total Devotion to God: Selected Writings of William Law*

Upper Room Books® website: books.upperroom.org

Cover design: Tim Green | Faceout Studio
Interior design and typesetting: PerfecType, Nashville, TN

ISBN 978-0-8358-1657-1 (print) | ISBN 978-0-8358-1697-7 (mobi) | ISBN 978-0-8358-1698-4 (epub)

Library of Congress Cataloging-in-Publication Data

Law, William, 1686–1761.
Total devotion to God: selected writings of William Law / selected, edited, and introduced by Keith Beasley-Topliffe.
p. cm.—(Upper Room spiritual classics. Series 3)
ISBN 0-8358-0901-3
1. Christian life—Anglican authors. I. Beasley-Topliffe, Keith. II. Title. III. Series.
BV4501.2.L3583 2000 99-37905
248.4'83—dc21 CIP

Contents

Introduction

For many Christians today, it is enough to be lukewarm in their devotion, as good a Christian as the next person. Anything more seems excessive, maybe even fanatical. We can become much more concerned with being saved than with figuring out what to do with the rest of our lives that Christ has redeemed.

William Law speaks against such an attitude in our day as he did in his own, two and a half centuries ago. Calmly, reasonably, he argues that only total devotion to God, dedication to holy living, is a proper response to God's love. If it is good to be good Christians, then surely it is excellent (not fanatical) to be excellent Christians. If we claim to follow Christ, why not follow him as well as we can?

In the following selections, taken from *A Serious Call to a Devout and Holy Life*, Law shows the importance of devotion. He argues that a disciplined life is by no means a dull or narrow one. He offers extensive suggestions for daily prayer that can shape the rest of one's life into one of praise for God and love for neighbor. Above all, he calls for religion that goes beyond duty to the outpouring of a God-filled heart.

Law's World

In the century and a half before Law's birth, England went through a great deal of political and religious conflict. King Henry VIII broke with Rome in 1532. However, his daughter Mary restored Catholicism in 1553 and executed many leaders of the English Reformation. Five years later her sister Elizabeth became queen, and England was again Protestant. During Elizabeth's forty-four-year reign, the Church of England became firmly entrenched.

When Elizabeth died in 1603, she was succeeded by her cousin James I, who was already king of Scotland. During his rule he authorized the translation of the Bible (1611) that commonly bears his name. He and his son, Charles I (reigned 1625–49), moved steadily toward returning to Roman Catholicism, even though they were the "supreme governors" of the Church of England. In 1649 the strongly Puritan Parliament raised its own army to overthrow and execute Charles. During the ten years of the English Commonwealth, the Church of England was disestablished (that is, was no longer the official government-supported church), and other Protestant groups such as Baptists and Quakers enjoyed toleration.

In 1660, Parliament restored the monarchy with Charles II as king. The Church of England was again established, and any group not abiding by the Book of Common Prayer could be liable to arrest. Many "nonconforming" ministers spent at least some time in prison. Among them were John Bunyan, who wrote much of *The Pilgrim's Progress* (published in 1678) while in jail.

Charles II was succeeded by his son James II in 1685. James openly embraced Roman Catholicism and was soon deposed in favor of his daughter Mary and her husband (and first cousin), William of Orange. Their reign began in 1689 with the Toleration Act, which allowed other Protestant groups freedom of religion as long as their ministers and meetinghouses were registered with the government. Although Catholics and Unitarians were not included, it was hoped that at last religious and political struggles were over.

One minority group displeased with the new rulers included nine Church of England bishops and several hundred clergy who felt their oaths of loyalty to James II could not be so easily swept away by an act of Parliament. They refused to swear a new oath to Mary and William and so lost the right to hold office in church or nation. These "nonjurors" (from Latin *jurare*, swear) formed a schismatic church that lasted more than a century.

Mary and her sister Anne (queen 1702–14) were at least descendants of James II. But William and Mary were childless, Anne's children died young, and other children of James II were excluded from the succession as Catholics. When Anne died, she was followed by George I, a German-born (and German-speaking) great-grandson of Charles I. Among those who refused the Oath of Allegiance to George (creating a new generation of nonjurors) was William Law.

One result of this religious and political fighting was a general distaste for any hint of extremism in religion. It was fine to attend worship and give something to charity now and then. But sufficient devotion to change one's life from the norm for one's class was at best in poor taste and at worst could become enthusiasm, a chargeable offense. Moderation was the key. Law took his stand against this attitude, calling instead for the pursuit of Christian perfection through a devout and holy life.

Another result was a philosophical quest for a common ground of religion through reason and study of human nature. Deism denied revelation (seeing Jesus as a natural philosopher) and denounced ritual as superstition. Law, on the other hand, insisted that devotion was a reasonable consequence of beginning any sort of religious life.

In Law's time, the class structure in England was firmly entrenched. One's class was a given, an instance of divine Providence. Law perceived class, wealth, and gender as one's state and therefore static, unchanging. Though Law was aware of the problems faced by the poor, he did not criticize the system at all. Instead, he counted on the charity of a devout upper class to ease the conditions of the lower classes.

Law's Life

William Law was born in 1686 in King's Cliffe, Northamptonshire, England. He was the fourth of eight children of Thomas

Law and his wife, Margaret. Thomas was the town grocer and sufficiently prosperous to be considered a gentleman.

In 1705, before he left home to study at Emmanuel College, Cambridge, Law drew up a set of rules for living that indicate severity and idealism were already part of his character. He graduated in 1708, became a fellow (instructor) at the college in 1711 and received his Master of Arts the next year. In 1714, when George I came to the throne, Law refused to take the Oath of Allegiance. As a nonjuror, Law was banned from teaching, from serving as a pastor in the Church of England, and from holding public office.

Law published his first pamphlet in 1717, the first of three open letters to the bishop of Bangor defending the nonjurors' positions. They were popular and brought Law some fame. He assured publication of these and other writings by giving the printer all profits from the first edition. Profit from later editions went to Law.

In 1723, Law became tutor to Edward Gibbon (father of historian Edward Gibbon, who wrote *The Decline and Fall of the Roman Empire*), both at the Gibbon home in Putney (near London) and at Emmanuel College when Gibbon went there. He remained part of the Gibbon household for the next fifteen years, long after Edward's studies were completed.

Law's writing continued with a major work on Christian perfection in 1726 followed two years later by *A Serious Call to a Devout and Holy Life, Adapted to the State and Condition of All Orders of Christians,* certainly his best-known work. Among those strongly influenced by this book were John and Charles Wesley, then beginning the group of devout students at Oxford that they called the Holy Club and detractors called Methodists. Both Wesleys visited and corresponded with Law.

About 1734, Law began reading the works of Jacob Boehme, called Behmen in the English editions of Law's day. Boehme (1575–1624) was a German shoemaker and mystic who claimed that his knowledge came not from study but from direct experience of God. Law found Boehme fascinating and integrated Boehme's mystical theology with his own practical devotion. Law's later works, such as *The Spirit of Prayer* (1749) and *The Spirit of Love* (1752), show the transformation Boehme made in Law's thought.

Law finally left the Gibbon home in 1738 and lived briefly in London before returning to King's Cliffe and the house his father had owned. Soon after Law moved there, Mrs. Elizabeth Hutcheson, widow of a member of Parliament, and Miss Hester Gibbon, older sister of Edward, asked Law to serve as their "chaplain, instructor, and almoner" (that is, to take charge of making charitable gifts on their behalf). At first the two women lived in a house several miles from King's Cliffe, but in 1744 they moved in with Law. There they tried to put into practice the devout life of which Law had written. Each woman was wealthy, with several thousand pounds of annual income probably far exceeding what Law earned from his writing. They gave away most (perhaps as much as 90 percent) of this income in direct charity and in support of two schools (one for boys and one for girls) and a library they established in King's Cliffe. The school buildings also included apartments for aged widows. Some of the neighbors complained that the copious amount of charity was bringing spongers into the community and placing Law in "competition" with the charity of the local parish church.

Law died in King's Cliffe on April 9, 1761, a few days after finishing *An Humble, Earnest, and Affectionate Address to the Clergy*, a renewed call for devotion and religious experience in contrast to overemphasis on reason and the pursuit of a ministerial career.

Further Reading

Many of Law's works are most easily available on the Internet. *A Serious Call* and some other works are also available in various print editions.

A. Keith Walker's *William Law: His Life and Thought* (SPCK, 1973) intermixes biography with critical summaries of Law's writings and was very helpful in preparing this introduction.

The Imitation of Christ by Thomas à Kempis (easily available in a variety of editions) strongly influenced Law's early spiritual formation. So did the writings of Nicolas Malebranche and Jeremy Taylor. Jacob Boehme's key writings were gathered in *The Way to Christ*, available in English from Paulist Press.

Note on the Text

All selections are from a 1906 edition of *A Serious Call* as reproduced in The AGES Digital Library CD-ROM, *The Master Christian Library*. The selections have been abridged (Law can become repetitive when driving home a point) and edited for punctuation, grammar, vocabulary, and inclusive language. Scripture quotes have been changed to the New Revised Standard Version.

Devout Life

From Chapter 1

William Law published A Serious Call to a Devout and Holy Life *in 1728. In these opening paragraphs, he defines what he means by a devout life.*

Devotion is neither private nor public prayer. But prayers, whether private or public, are particular parts or instances of devotion. Devotion signifies a life given or devoted to God.

Devout people, therefore, live no longer according to their own will or the way and spirit of the world but solely according to the will of God. They consider God in everything, serve God in everything, make all the parts of their ordinary lives parts of their piety by doing everything in the name of God and under such rules as conform to God's glory.

We readily acknowledge that God alone is to be the rule and measure of our prayers. In them we are to look wholly to God and act wholly for God. We are to pray only in such a manner, for such things, and for such ends as are suitable to God's glory.

Now let any find out the reason why they are to be strictly pious in their prayers, and they will find the same as strong a reason to be as strictly pious in all the other parts of their lives. For there is no other reason why our prayers should be according to the will of God, why they should have nothing in them but what is wise, and holy, and heavenly than this: that our lives may be of the same nature, full of the same wisdom, holiness, and heavenly tempers, and that we may live to God in the same spirit that we pray to God. Were it not our strict duty to live by reason and to devote all the actions of our lives to God, were it not absolutely necessary to walk before God in wisdom and holiness and all heavenly conversation, doing everything in God's name and for God's glory, there would be no excellency or wisdom in the most heavenly prayers. No, such prayers would be absurdities. They would be like prayers for wings when it was no part of our duty to fly.

It is for lack of knowing or at least considering this that we see such a mixture of the ridiculous in the lives of many people. You see them strict as to some times and places of devotion. But when the church service is over, they are just like those who seldom or never come there. In their way of life, their manner of spending their time and money, their cares and fears, their pleasures and indulgences, their labor and diversions, they are like the rest of the world. This makes the loose part of the world generally make a joke of those who are devout because they see their devotion goes no farther than their prayers, and that when they are over, they live no more to God till the time of prayer returns again. Instead they live by the same humor and fancy and in as full enjoyment of all the follies of life as other people. This is the reason why they are the joke and scorn of careless and worldly people: not because they are really devoted to God, but because they appear to have no other devotion but that of occasional prayers.

And indeed nothing can be imagined more absurd in itself than wise and sublime and heavenly prayers added to a life of vanity and folly, where neither labor nor diversions, neither time nor money, are under the direction of the wisdom and heavenly tempers of our prayers. If we were to see a man claiming to act wholly with regard to God in everything that he did, who would neither spend time nor money nor take any labor or diversion but so far as he could act according to strict principles of reason and piety, and yet at the same time neglect all prayer, public or private, should we not be amazed at such a man and wonder how he could have so much folly along with so much religion?

Yet this is as reasonable as for any person to claim strictness in devotion, to be careful in observing times and places of prayer, and yet letting the rest of his life, his time and labor, his talents and money, be disposed of without any regard to strict rules of piety and devotion. For it is as great an absurdity to suppose holy prayers and divine petitions without a holiness of life suitable to them, as to suppose a holy and divine life without prayers.

The short of the matter is this: either reason and religion prescribe rules and ends to all the ordinary actions of our lives, or they do not. If they do, then it is as necessary to govern all our actions by those rules as it is to worship God. For if religion teaches us anything concerning eating and drinking or spending our time and money; if it teaches us how we are to have contempt for the world; if it tells us what tempers we are to have in common life, how we are to be disposed toward all people, and how we are to behave toward the sick, the poor, the old, the destitute; if it tells us whom we are to treat with a particular love or to regard with a particular esteem; if it tells us how we are to treat our enemies and how we are to mortify and deny ourselves; then they must be very weak that can think these parts of religion are not to be observed with as much exactness as any doctrines that relate to prayers.

Seeking Perfection

From Chapter 3

Here Law suggests that meditating on the virtues we would like to have at the hour of death will guide us to seek them now.

The measure of our love to God seems in justice to be the measure of our love of every virtue. We are to love and practice it with all our hearts, with all our souls, with all our minds, and with all our strength. And when we cease to live with this regard to virtue, we live below our nature. Instead of being able to plead our infirmities, we stand chargeable with negligence.

It is for this reason that we are exhorted to work out our salvation with fear and trembling. Unless our hearts and passions are eagerly bent upon the work of our salvation; unless holy fears animate our endeavors and keep our consciences strict and tender about every part of our duty, constantly examining how we live and how fit we are to die; we shall in all probability fall into a state of negligence and sit down in such a course of life as will never carry us to the rewards of heaven.

And whoever considers that a just God can make such allowances only as are suitable to divine justice, that our works are all to be examined by fire, will find that fear and trembling are proper tempers for those who are drawing near so great a trial.

And indeed there is no probability that any should do all the duty that God expects or make the progress in piety that the holiness and justice of God require but those who are constantly afraid of falling short of it.

Now this is not intended to possess people's minds with a scrupulous anxiety and discontent in the service of God but to fill them with a just fear of living in sloth and idleness and in the neglect of such virtues as they will want at the day of judgment. It is to excite them to an earnest examination of their lives, to such zeal and care and concern for Christian perfection as they use in any matter that has gained their hearts and affections. It is only desiring them to be so apprehensive of their state, so humble in the opinion of themselves, so earnest after higher degrees of piety, and so fearful of falling short of happiness as the great apostle Saint Paul was, when he wrote to the Philippians: "Not that I have already obtained this or have already reached the goal; . . . but this one thing I do: forgetting what lies behind and straining forward to what lies ahead, I press on toward the goal for the prize of the heavenly call of God in Christ Jesus." And then he added, "Let those of us then who are mature be of the same mind."

The Apostle thought it necessary for those who were in his state of perfection to be "of the same mind," that is, laboring, pressing, and aspiring after some degree of holiness to which they had not then arrived. Surely it is much more necessary for us, who are laboring under great imperfections, to be earnest and striving after such degrees of a holy and divine life as we have not yet attained.

The best way for any to know how much they ought to aspire after holiness is to consider not how much will make their present lives easy, but how much they think will make them easy at the hour of death.

Now any who dare be so serious as to put this question to themselves will be forced to answer that at death all will wish that they had been as perfect as human nature can be.

Is not this, therefore, sufficient to put us not only upon wishing, but laboring after all the perfection that we shall then lament the lack of? Is it not excessive folly to be content with such a course of piety as we already know cannot content us at a time when we shall so desire it as to have nothing else to comfort us? How can we carry a severer condemnation against ourselves than to believe that at the hour of death, we shall want the virtues of the saints and wish that we had been among the first servants of God and yet take no methods of arriving at their height of piety while we are alive?

This is an absurdity that we can easily pass over at present, while the health of our bodies, the passions of our minds, the noise and hurry and pleasures and business of the world lead us on with eyes that see not and ears that hear not. But at death, it will set itself before us in a dreadful magnitude. It will haunt us like a dismal ghost, and the conscience will never let us take our eyes from it.

We see in worldly matters what a torment self-condemnation is, and how hardly any are able to forgive themselves when they have brought themselves into any calamity or disgrace purely by their own folly. The affliction is made doubly tormenting because they are forced to charge it all to themselves, as their own acts and deeds against the nature and reason of things and contrary to the advice of all their friends.

Now from this we may in some degree guess how terrible the pain of that self-condemnation will be when any shall find themselves in the miseries of death under the severity of a self-condemning conscience, charging all their distress to their own folly and madness against the sense and reason of their own minds, against all the doctrines and precepts of religion, and contrary to all the instructions, calls, and warnings of both God and people.

Business

From Chapter 4

Law often presents character sketches as either positive or negative examples. Often the character's name helps to understand the portrait. Here Calidus (Latin for hot*) is so hot to get ahead in business that he has little time for God except during business emergencies.*

Calidus has traded more than thirty years in the greatest city of the kingdom. He has been so many years constantly increasing his trade and his fortune. Every hour of the day is with him an hour of business. Though he eats and drinks very heartily, yet every meal seems to be in a hurry. He would say grace if he had time. Calidus ends every day at the tavern though he is not free to be there until nearly nine o'clock. He is always forced to drink a good hearty glass to drive thoughts of business out of his head and make his spirits drowsy enough for sleep. He does business all the time that he is rising and has settled several matters before he can get to his counting room. His prayers are a short ejaculation or two. He never misses them in stormy, tempestuous weather because he has always something or other at sea. Calidus will tell you with great pleasure that he has been in this hurry for many years, and that it might have killed him long ago, except that it has been a rule with him to get out of town every Saturday and make Sunday a day of quiet and good refreshment in the country.

He is now so rich that he would leave off his business and amuse his old age with building and furnishing a fine house in the country. But he is afraid he should grow melancholy if he quit his business. He will tell you with great gravity that it is a dangerous thing for a man who has been used to getting money ever to stop. If thoughts of religion happen at any time to steal into his head, Calidus contents himself with thinking that he never was a friend to heretics and infidels, that he has always been civil to the minister of his parish, and that he has very often given something to the charity schools.

Now this way of life is at such a distance from all the doctrine and discipline of Christianity that no one can live in it through ignorance or frailty. Calidus can no more imagine that he is born again of the Spirit; that he is a new creation in Christ; that he lives here as an alien and exile, setting his mind on things above and laying up treasures in heaven—he can no more imagine this than he can think that he has been all his life an apostle, working miracles and preaching the gospel.

It must be admitted that businesspeople in general, especially in great towns, are too much like Calidus. You see them all the week buried in business, unable to think of anything else. Then they spend Sunday in idleness and refreshment, in wandering into the country, in such visits and jovial meetings as make it often the worst day of the week.

Now they do not live like this because they cannot support themselves with less care and application to business but because they want to grow rich in their trades and to maintain their families in some such figure and degree of finery as a reasonable Christian life has no occasion for. Take away this temper and then people of all trades will find themselves at leisure to live every day like Christians, to be careful of every duty of the gospel, to live in a visible course of religion, and to be every day strict observers of both private and public prayer.

Now the only way to do this is for people to consider their trade as something they are obliged to devote to the glory of God, something they are to do only in such a manner that they may make it a duty to God. Nothing can be right in business that is not under these rules.

It is therefore absolutely certain that no Christians are to enter any farther into business, or for any other ends, than such as they can in singleness of heart offer to God as a reasonable service. For the Son of God has redeemed us for this end only: that we should, by a life of reason and piety, live to the glory of God. This is the only rule and measure for every order and state of life. Without this rule, the most lawful employment becomes a sinful state of life.

Miranda's Life

From Chapter 8

The centerpiece of the first half of A Serious Call *is the portrait of Miranda, whose name means* wonderful. *She and her sister Flavia (*extravagant*) are women who have maintained their independence by remaining single and living on endowment income. But while Flavia wastes her wealth on self-centered indulgence, Miranda is a model of Christian charity and devotion.*

Miranda is a sober, reasonable Christian. As soon as she was mistress of her time and fortune, her first thought was how she might best fulfill everything that God required of her in the use of them and how she might make the best and happiest use of this short life. She depends upon the truth of what our blessed Lord has said, that "there is need of only one thing," and therefore makes her whole life one continual labor after it. She has only one reason for doing or not doing, for liking or not liking anything, and that is the will of God. She is not so weak as to pretend to add what is called the fine lady to the true Christian. Miranda thinks too well to be taken with the sound of such silly words. She has renounced the world to follow Christ in the exercise of humility, charity, devotion, abstinence, and heavenly affections. That is Miranda's fine breeding.

While she was under her mother, she was forced to be genteel, to live in ceremony, to sit up late at nights, to be in the folly of every fashion, and to always visit on Sundays. She was forced to go patched and loaded with a burden of finery to the Holy Sacrament, to be in every polite conversation, to hear profanity at the playhouse and wanton songs and love intrigues at the opera, and to dance at public places so that fops and rakes might admire the fineness of her shape and the beauty of her motions. The remembrance of this way of life makes her exceedingly careful to atone for it by a contrary behavior.

Miranda does not divide her duty between God, her neighbor, and herself. She considers all as due to God. So she does everything in God's name and for God's sake. This makes her consider her fortune as the gift of God that is to be used, as is everything that belongs to God, for the wise and reasonable ends of a Christian and holy life. Her fortune, therefore, is divided between herself and several poor people, and she has only her part of relief from it. She thinks it the same folly to indulge herself in needless, vain expenses as to give to other people to spend in the same way. Therefore as she will not give a poor man money to see a puppet show, neither will she allow herself any to spend in the same manner. She thinks it very proper to be as wise as she expects poor men should be. For it is a folly and a crime in a poor man, says Miranda, to waste what is given him in foolish trifles, while he lacks meat, drink, and clothes. And is it less folly or less a crime in me to spend that money in silly diversions that might be so much better spent in imitation of the divine goodness, in works of kindness and charity toward my fellow creatures and fellow Christians?

Except for her food, she never spent as much as ten pounds a year upon herself. If you were to see her, you would wonder what poor body it was that was so surprisingly neat and clean. She has but one rule that she observes in her dress: to be always clean and in the cheapest things. Everything about her resembles the purity of her soul. She is always clean without, because she is always pure within.

Every morning sees her early at her prayers. She rejoices in the beginning of every day because it begins all her pious rules of holy living and brings the fresh pleasure of repeating them. She seems to be as a guardian angel to those who dwell about her. With her prayers she blesses the place where she dwells and makes intercession with God for those who are asleep.

When you see her at work, you see the same wisdom that governs all her other actions. She is doing something that is necessary for herself or necessary for others who want to be assisted. There is scarcely a poor family in the neighborhood that does not wear something or other that has had the labor of her hands. Her wise and pious mind neither wants the amusement nor can bear with the folly of idle and impertinent work. She can allow no such folly as this by day because she has to answer for all her actions at night. When there is no wisdom to be observed in the employment of her hands, when there is no useful or charitable work to be done, Miranda will work no more. At her table she lives strictly by this rule of Holy Scripture, "Whether you eat or drink, or whatever you do, do everything for the glory of God." This makes her begin and end every meal as she begins and ends every day: with acts of devotion. She eats and drinks only for the sake of living. With such regular abstinence every meal is an exercise of self-denial. She humbles her body every time that she is forced to feed it. If Miranda were to run a race for her life, she would submit to a diet that was proper for it. But since the race set before her is a race of holiness, purity, and heavenly affection that she is to finish in a corrupt, disordered body of earthly passions, so her everyday diet has only this one end: to make her body fitter for this spiritual race.

The Holy Scriptures, especially the New Testament, are her daily study. She reads them with watchful attention, constantly casting an eye upon herself and trying herself by every doctrine that is there. When she has the New Testament in her hand, she supposes herself at the feet of our Savior and his apostles and makes everything that she learns of them so many laws of her life. She receives their sacred words with as much attention and reverence as if she saw their persons and knew that they were just come from heaven to teach her the way that leads to it.

She is sometimes afraid that she pays too much money for books because she cannot forbear buying all practical books of any note, especially such as enter into the heart of religion and describe the inward holiness of the Christian life. But of all human writings the lives of pious persons and eminent saints are her greatest delight. She searches them as for hidden treasure, hoping to find some secret of holy living, some uncommon degree of piety she may make her own. By this means Miranda has her head and her heart so stored with all the principles of wisdom and holiness, she is so full of the one main business of life, that she finds it difficult to converse upon any other subject. If you are in her company when she thinks it proper to talk, you must be made wiser and better, whether you will or no.

Miranda's Charity

From Chapter 8

After describing Miranda's personal conduct, he turns to her use of money for charitable purposes.

To tell of her charity would be to relate the history of every day for twenty years. For so long her fortune has all been spent that way. She has set up about twenty poor tradesmen who had failed in their businesses and saved as many from failing. She has educated several poor children and put them in a way of honest employment. As soon as any laborer is confined at home with sickness, she sends him, until he recovers, twice the value of his wages so that he may have one part to give to his family as usual and the other to provide things needed for his sickness.

If a family seems too large to be supported by the labor of those who can work in it, she pays their rent and gives them something yearly toward their clothing. By this means, there are several poor families that live in a comfortable manner and are from year to year blessing her in their prayers.

If any poor men or women are more than ordinarily wicked and reprobate, Miranda has her eye upon them. She watches their time of need and adversity. And if she can discover that they are in any great straits or affliction, she gives them speedy relief. She has this care for this sort of people because she once saved a very dissolute person from being carried to prison, who immediately became a true penitent.

There is nothing in the character of Miranda more to be admired than this temper. For this tenderness of affection toward the most abandoned sinners is the highest example of a divine and godlike soul.

Miranda is a constant relief to poor people in their misfortunes and accidents. There are sometimes little misfortunes that happen to them that they could never be able to overcome by themselves. The death of a cow or a horse or some little robbery would keep them in distress all their lives. She does not allow them to grieve under such accidents. She immediately gives them the full value of their loss and makes use of it as a means of raising their minds toward God.

She has a great tenderness for older people who have grown past their labor. The parish allowance to such people is very seldom a comfortable maintenance. For this reason they are the constant objects of her care. She adds so much to their allowance as to exceed the wages they got when they were young. This she does to comfort the infirmities of their age so that, being free from trouble and distress, they may serve God in peace and tranquillity of mind. She has generally a large number of this kind who, by her charities and exhortations to holiness, spend their last days in great piety and devotion.

Miranda never wants for compassion, even for common beggars—especially those who are old or sick or full of sores or lack eyes or limbs. She hears their complaints with tenderness, gives them some proof of her kindness, and never rejects them with hard or reproachful language for fear of adding affliction to her fellow creatures.

It may be, says Miranda, that I may often give to those who do not deserve it or who will make an ill use of my alms. But what then? Is not this the very method of divine goodness? Does not God make the "sun rise on the evil and on the good"? Is not this the very goodness that is recommended to us in Scripture, that, by imitating it, we may be children of our Father in heaven, who "sends rain on the righteous and on the unrighteous"? And shall I withhold a little money or food from my fellow creature for fear he should not be good enough to receive it of me? Do I beg of God to deal with me not according to my merit but according to God's own great goodness; and shall I be so absurd as to withhold my charity from a poor brother because he may perhaps not deserve it? Shall I use a measure toward him that I pray God never to use toward me?

Besides, where has the Scripture made merit the rule or measure of charity? On the contrary, the Scripture says, "If your enemies are hungry, feed them; if they are thirsty, give them something to drink."

Now this plainly teaches us that the merit of persons is to be no rule of our charity. We are to do acts of kindness to those that least of all deserve it. For if I am to love and do good to my worst enemies and be charitable to them despite all their malice, surely merit is no measure of charity. If I am not to withhold my charity from such bad people who are at the same time my enemies, surely I am not to deny alms to poor beggars whom I know to be neither bad people nor any way my enemies.

You will perhaps say that by this means I encourage people to be beggars. But the same thoughtless objection may be made against all kinds of charities, since they may encourage people to depend upon them. The same may be said against forgiving our enemies, for it may encourage people to do us hurt. The same may be said even against the goodness of God: by pouring blessings on the evil and on the good, on the unjust and on the just, evil and unjust people are encouraged in their wicked ways. The same may be said against clothing the naked or giving medicine to the sick: that may encourage people to neglect themselves and be careless of their health. But when the love of God dwells in you, when it has enlarged your heart and filled you with mercy and compassion, you will make no more such objections.

This is the spirit and life of the devout Miranda. When she dies, she must shine among apostles and saints and martyrs. She must stand among the first servants of God and be glorious among those who have fought the good fight and finished their course with joy.

Prayer and Devotion

From Chapter 10

After the special case of Miranda, Law goes on to argue that devotion, like prayer, is for all people in any walk of life.

It is granted that prayer is a duty that belongs to all states and conditions of people. If we inquire into the reason why no state of life is to be excused from prayer, we shall find it as good a reason why every state of life is to be made a state of piety and holiness in all its parts.

For we pray and glorify God with hymns and psalms of thanksgiving because we are to live wholly for God and glorify God in all possible ways. It is not because the praises of words or forms of thanksgiving are more particularly parts of piety or more the worship of God than other things. But it is because they are possible ways of expressing our dependence, our obedience, and our devotion to God. Now if the reason for verbal praises and thanksgiving to God is that we are to live for God in all possible ways, then it plainly follows that we are equally obliged to worship and glorify God in all other actions that can be turned into acts of piety and obedience to God. And as actions are of much more significance than words, it must be a much more acceptable worship to glorify God in all the actions of our common life than with any little form of words at any particular times.

Thus, if God is to be worshiped with forms of thanksgiving, those who make it a rule to be content and thankful in every part and accident of life, because it comes from God, praise God in a much higher manner than those who have some set time for singing psalms. Those who dare not say an ill-natured word or do an unreasonable thing because they consider God as everywhere present perform a better devotion than those who dare not miss church. Living in the world as a stranger and a pilgrim, using all its enjoyments as if we used them not and making all our actions so many steps toward a better life, is offering a better sacrifice to God than any forms of holy and heavenly prayers.

To be humble in all our actions, to avoid every appearance of pride and vanity, to be meek and lowly in our words, actions, dress, behavior, and designs, in imitation of our blessed Savior, is to worship God in a higher manner than those who have only certain times to fall low on their knees in devotions. Those who content themselves with necessities in order to give the remainder to those that lack it and who dare not to spend any money foolishly, considering it as a talent from God that must be used according to God's will, praise God with something that is more glorious than songs of praise.

Those who have appointed times for the use of wise and pious prayers perform a proper instance of devotion. But those who allow themselves no times or places or actions but those strictly conformable to wisdom and holiness worship the Divine nature with the most true and substantial devotion. For who does not know that it is better to be pure and holy than to talk about purity and holiness? No, who does not know that people are to be reckoned no more pure or holy or just than they are pure and holy and just in the common course of their lives? But if this is plain, then it is also plain that it is better to be holy than to have holy prayers.

Prayers, therefore, are so far from being a sufficient devotion that they are the smallest parts of it. We are to praise God with words and prayers because such praise is a possible way of glorifying God. But then as words are but small things in themselves and times of prayer are but little if compared with the rest of our lives, so devotion that consists in times and forms of prayer is but a very small thing if compared to devotion that appears in every other part and circumstance of our lives.

Bended knees, while you are clothed with pride; heavenly petitions, while you are hoarding up treasures upon earth; holy devotions, while you live in the follies of the world; prayers of meekness and charity, while your heart is the seat of pride and resentment; hours of prayer, while you give up days and years to idle diversions, impertinent visits, and foolish pleasures—all are as absurd and unacceptable services to God as forms of thanksgiving from a person who lives in moping and discontent.

Unless the common course of our lives is according to the common spirit of our prayers, our prayers are so far from being a real or sufficient degree of devotion that they become an empty lip service or, what is worse, a notorious hypocrisy.

Since we are to make the spirit and temper of our prayers the common spirit and temper of our lives, this may convince us that all orders of people are to labor and aspire after the same utmost perfection of the Christian life. For as all Christians are to use the same holy and heavenly devotions and with the same earnestness to pray for the Spirit of God, so is it a sufficient proof that all orders of people are, to the utmost of their power, to make their lives agreeable to the one Spirit for whom they are all to pray.

Discipline

From Chapter 11

In this selection Law addresses the concern that following Christian disciplines in our lives will make them boring and uncomfortable.

Most people confess that religion preserves us from a great many evils and helps us in many respects to a more happy enjoyment of ourselves. But then they imagine that this is true only of such a moderate share of religion as gently restrains us from the excesses of our passions. They suppose that the strict rules and restraints of an exalted piety are such contradictions to our nature as must make our lives dull and uncomfortable.

This objection supposes that religion, moderately practiced, adds much to the happiness of life but that such heights of piety as the perfection of religion requires have a contrary effect.

It supposes, therefore, that it is happy to be kept from the excesses of envy, but unhappy to be kept from other degrees of envy. That it is happy to be delivered from a boundless ambition, but unhappy to be without a more moderate ambition. It supposes, also, that the happiness of life consists in a mixture of virtue and vice, a mixture of ambition and humility, charity and envy, heavenly affection and covetousness. All this is as absurd as to suppose that it is happy to be free from excessive pains, but unhappy to be without more moderate pains; or that the happiness of health consists in being partly sick and partly well.

If religion restrains only the excesses of revenge but lets the spirit still live within you in lesser instances, your religion may have made your life a little more outwardly decent but not made you at all happier or easier in yourself. But if you have once sacrificed all thoughts of revenge in obedience to God and are resolved to return good for evil at all times in order to render yourself more like God and fitter for God's mercy in the kingdom of love and glory, this is a height of virtue that will make you feel its happiness.

Piety requires us to renounce no ways of life where we can act reasonably and offer what we do to the glory of God. All ways of life—all satisfactions and enjoyments—that are within these bounds are no way denied us by the strictest rules of piety. Whatever you can do or enjoy as in the presence of God, as God's servant, as God's rational creature that has received reason and knowledge from God, and all that you can do in conformity to a rational nature and the will of God—all this is allowed by the laws of piety. Will you think that your life will be uncomfortable unless you may displease God, be a fool, and act contrary to the reason and wisdom that God has implanted in you?

As for those satisfactions we dare not offer to a holy God, that are invented only by the folly and corruption of the world, that inflame our passions and sink our souls into grossness and sensuality and render us incapable of the Divine favor either here or hereafter—surely it can be no uncomfortable state of life to be rescued by religion from such self-murder and to be rendered capable of eternal happiness.

Let us suppose a person destitute of the knowledge we have from our senses, placed somewhere alone by himself in the midst of a variety of things he did not know how to use: bread, wine, water, gold dust, iron chains, gravel, garments, fire, etc. Let us suppose that he has no knowledge of the right use of these things or any direction from his senses how to quench his thirst or satisfy his hunger or make any use of the things about him. In his thirst, he puts gold dust into his eyes. When his eyes smart, he puts wine into his ears. In his hunger, he puts gravel into his mouth. In pain, he loads himself with the iron chains. Feeling cold, he puts his feet in the water. Being frightened by the fire, he runs away from it. Being weary, he makes a seat of his bread. Through his ignorance of the right use of the things that are about him, he will vainly torment himself while he lives and at last die, blinded with dust, choked with gravel, and loaded with irons. Let us suppose that some good being came to him and showed him the nature and use of all the things that were about him and gave him such strict rules of using them as would certainly, if observed, make him the happier for all that he had and deliver him from the pains of hunger and thirst and cold.

Now could you with any reason affirm that those strict rules of using those things that were about him had rendered that poor man's life dull and uncomfortable?

Now this is in some measure a representation of the strict rules of religion. They only relieve our ignorance, save us from tormenting ourselves, and teach us to use everything about us to our proper advantage.

We are placed in a world full of a variety of things. Our ignorance makes us use many of them as absurdly as the man who put dust in his eyes to relieve his thirst or put on chains to remove pain.

Religion, therefore, comes in to our relief and gives us strict rules of using all things that are about us, so that by using them suitably to our own nature and the nature of the things we may have always the pleasure of receiving a right benefit from them.

Seeing Clearly

From Chapter 13

Law hopes that by careful observation of the people and events around them, people will be inspired to change their lives, just as well-born Eugenius is shocked into repentance by the death of Octavius.

Let us only intend to see and hear, and then the whole world becomes a book of wisdom and instruction to us. All that is regular in the order of nature, all that is accidental in the course of things, all the mistakes and disappointments that happen to us, and all the miseries and errors that we see in other people become so many plain lessons of advice to us. They teach us, with as much assurance as an angel from heaven, that we can in no way raise ourselves to any true happiness but by turning all our thoughts, wishes, and endeavors after the happiness of another life.

It is this right use of the world that I would lead you into by directing you to turn your eyes upon every shape of human folly. From that you may draw fresh arguments and motives of living to the best and greatest purposes of your creation.

If you would only carry with you this intention of profiting by the follies of the world and of learning the greatness of religion from the littleness and vanity of every other way of life, you would find every day, every place, and every person, a fresh proof of the wisdom of those who choose to live wholly to God. You would then often return home the wiser, the better, and the more strengthened in religion by everything that has fallen in your way.

Octavius is a learned, ingenious man, well versed in most parts of literature and no stranger to any kingdom in Europe. The other day, being just recovered from a lingering fever, he began to talk thus to his friends: "My glass is almost run out, and your eyes see how many marks of age and death I bear. I plainly feel myself sinking away faster than any bystanders imagine. I fully believe that one year more will conclude my reckoning."

The attention of his friends was much raised by such a declaration. They expected to hear something truly excellent from so learned a man, who had only a year longer to live. Octavius proceeded in this manner: "For these reasons, my friends, I have left off all taverns. The wine of those places is not good enough for me in this decay of nature. I must now be particular in what I drink. I cannot pretend to do as I have done and therefore am resolved to furnish my own cellar with a little of the very best, though it cost me ever so much.

"I must also tell you, my friends, that age forces a man to be wise in many other respects and makes us change many of our opinions and practices.

"You know how much I have liked a large acquaintance. I now condemn it as an error. Three or four cheerful, diverting companions are all that I now desire. I find that in my present infirmities if I am left alone or to solemn company, I am not so easy to myself."

A few days after Octavius had made this declaration to his friends, he relapsed into his former illness and was committed to a nurse, who closed his eyes before his fresh parcel of wine came in.

Young Eugenius, who was present at this discourse, went home a new man, with full resolutions of devoting himself wholly to God.

"I never," says Eugenius, "was so deeply affected with the wisdom and importance of religion as when I saw how poorly and meanly the learned Octavius was to leave the world through the lack of it.

"How often I had envied his great learning, his skill in languages, his knowledge of antiquity, his address, and his fine manner of expressing himself upon all subjects! But when I saw how poorly it all ended, what was to be the last year of such a life, and how foolishly the master of all these accomplishments was then forced to talk, for lack of being acquainted with the joys and expectations of piety, I was thoroughly convinced that there was nothing to be envied or desired but a life of true piety, nor anything so poor and comfortless as a death without it."

Young Eugenius was thus edified and instructed in the present case. If you are so fortunate as to have anything of his thoughtful temper, you will meet with variety of instruction of this kind. You will find that arguments for the wisdom and happiness of a strict piety offer themselves in all places and appeal to all your senses in the plainest manner.

You will find that all the world preaches to an attentive mind. If you have but ears to hear, almost everything you meet teaches you some lesson of wisdom.

But now, if to these admonitions and instructions that we receive from our senses and from an experience of the state of human life—if to these we add the lights of religion, those great truths the Son of God has taught us, it will be then as much beyond all doubt that there is but one happiness for a person, as that there is but one God.

For since religion teaches us that our souls are immortal, that piety and devotion will carry them to an eternal enjoyment of God, and that carnal, worldly tempers will sink them into an everlasting misery with damned spirits, what gross nonsense and stupidity it is to give the name of joy or happiness to anything but what carries us to this joy and happiness in God!

Negotius

From Chapter 13

In the portrait of Negotius (businessman), *Law hopes to show how being a good, sober, honest person is not the same as being devout and how true devotion and business might go together.*

Negotius is a temperate, honest man. He served his time under a master of great trade but has, by his own management, made it a more substantial business than ever it was before. The general good of trade seems to Negotius to be the general good of life. Whom he admires or what he commends or condemns, either in church or in state, is admired, commended, or condemned with some regard to trade.

As money is continually pouring in upon him, so he often lets it go in various kinds of expense and generosity, sometimes in ways of charity.

He has given a fine set of bells to a church in the country. There is much expectation that he will some time or other make a more beautiful front to the markethouse than has yet been seen in any place. For it is the generous spirit of Negotius to do nothing in a cheap way.

If you ask what has secured Negotius from all scandalous vices, it is the same thing that has kept him from all strictness of devotion: his great business. He has always had too many important things in his head to allow him either to fall into any courses of debauchery or to feel the necessity of an inward, solid piety.

For this reason he hears of the pleasures of debauchery and the pleasures of piety with the same indifference. He has no more desire of living in the one than in the other because neither of them consists with that turn of mind and multiplicity of business that are his happiness.

If Negotius were asked what he drives at in life, he would be as much at a loss for an answer as if he were asked what any other person is thinking. For though he always seems to himself to know what he is doing and has many things in his head that are the motives of his actions, yet he cannot tell you of any one general end in life that he has chosen with deliberation as being truly worthy of all his labor and pains. The thing that seems to give Negotius the greatest life and spirit and to be most in his thoughts is an expectation that he shall die richer than any of his business ever did.

Most people, when they think of happiness, think of Negotius, in whose life every instance of happiness is supposed to meet. He is sober, prudent, rich, prosperous, generous, and charitable.

Let us now, therefore, look at this condition in another, but truer light.

Suppose that this same Negotius was a painstaking, hard-working man, every day deep in a variety of affairs, and that he neither drank nor debauched but was sober and regular in his business. Suppose that he grew old in this course of trading and that the end and design of all this labor, and care, and application to business was only this: that he might die possessed of more than one hundred thousand pairs of boots and spurs.

Now if this were really the case, I believe it would be readily granted that a life of such business was as poor and ridiculous as any that can be invented. But it would puzzle anyone to show that people who have spent all their time and thoughts in business and hurry that they might die, as it is said, worth one hundred thousand pounds are any wiser than one who has taken the same pains to have as many pairs of boots and spurs when he leaves the world.

For the only end of life is to die as free from sin and exalted in virtue as we can. Naked we came and naked we are to return and to stand trial before Christ and his holy angels for everlasting happiness or misery. Then what can it possibly signify what we had or did not have in this world? What can it signify what we call the things that we leave behind, whether we call them one hundred thousand pounds or one hundred thousand pairs of boots and spurs?

Now it is easy to see the folly of a life spent to furnish a man with such a number of boots and spurs. For when he has got all his boots, his soul is to go to its own place among separate spirits and his body be laid by in a coffin till the last trumpet calls him to judgment. There the inquiry will be how humbly, how devoutly, how purely, how meekly, how piously, how charitably, how heavenly we have spoken, thought, and acted while we were in the body. How can we say that those who have worn out their lives in raising one hundred thousand pounds have acted wiser than one who has had the same care to procure one hundred thousand of anything else?

But suppose that Negotius, when he first entered into business, happened to read the gospel with attention and eyes open and found that he had a much greater business on his hands than that to which he had served an apprenticeship. Suppose that he had discovered that his soul was more to him than his body; that it was better to grow in the virtues of the soul than to have a large body or a full purse; better to be fit for heaven than to have a variety of fine houses upon the earth; better to secure everlasting happiness than to have plenty of things that he cannot keep; better to live in habits of humility, piety, devotion, charity, and self-denial than to die unprepared for judgment; better to be most like our Savior or some eminent saint than to excel all the tradesmen in the world in business and bulk of fortune. Suppose that Negotius, believing these things to be true, entirely devoted himself to God at his first setting out in the world, resolving to pursue his business no farther than was consistent with great devotion, humility, and self-denial and for no other ends but to provide himself with a sober subsistence and to do all the good that he could to the souls and bodies of his fellow creatures.

Suppose, therefore, that instead of the continual hurry of business, he was frequent in his retirements and a strict observer of all the hours of prayer; that, instead of restless desires after more riches, his soul had been full of the love of God and heavenly affection, constantly watching against worldly tempers and always aspiring after divine grace; that, instead of worldly cares and contrivances, he was busy in fortifying his soul against all approaches of sin; that, instead of costly show and expensive generosity of a splendid life, he loved and exercised all instances of humility and lowliness; that, instead of great treats and full tables, his house furnished only sober refreshment to those who wanted it. Let it be supposed that his contentment kept him free from all kinds of envy; that his piety made him thankful to God in all crosses and disappointments; that his charity kept him from being rich by a continual distribution to all objects of compassion. Now, had this been the Christian spirit of Negotius, can anyone say that he had lost the true joy and happiness of life by thus conforming to the spirit and living up to the hopes of the gospel? Can it be said that a life made exemplary by such virtues as these that keep heaven always in our sight, that both delight and exalt the soul here and prepare it for the presence of God hereafter, must be poor and dull if compared to that of heaping up riches that can neither stay with us nor we with them?

Soul and Body

From Chapter 15

In the last half of A Serious Call, *Law writes about topics for prayer throughout the day. The first topic, for prayer on rising at 6:00 a.m., is praise. After giving examples of spoken prayers, he urges readers to begin by singing or chanting a psalm so that the body joins the mind in prayer.*

The soul and the body are so united that each has power over the other in its actions. Certain thoughts and sentiments in the soul produce such and such motions and actions in the body. On the other hand, certain motions and actions of the body have the same power of raising such and such thoughts and sentiments in the soul. As singing is the natural effect of joy in the mind, so it is as truly a natural cause of raising joy in the mind.

As devotion of the heart naturally breaks out into outward acts of prayer, so outward acts of prayer are natural means of raising the devotion of the heart.

If we simply consider human nature, we shall find that singing or chanting psalms is as proper and necessary to raise our hearts to a delight in God as prayer is proper and necessary to excite in us the spirit of devotion. Every reason for one is in all respects as strong a reason for the other.

If, therefore, you would know the reason and necessity of singing psalms, you must consider the reason and necessity of praising and rejoicing in God. Singing psalms is as much the true exercise and support of the spirit of thanksgiving as prayer is the true exercise and support of the spirit of devotion. You may as well think that you can be devout as you ought without the use of prayer as that you can rejoice in God as you ought without the practice of singing psalms. This singing is as much the natural language of praise and thanksgiving as prayer is the natural language of devotion.

This union of our souls and bodies is the reason both why we have so little and why we have so much power over ourselves. It is owing to this union that we have so little power over our souls. We cannot prevent the effects of external objects upon our bodies or command outward causes. So we cannot always command the inward state of our minds. As outward objects act upon our bodies without our leave, so our bodies act upon our minds by the laws of the union of the soul and the body. So you see it is owing to this union that we have so little power over ourselves.

On the other hand, it is owing to this union that we have so much power over ourselves. Our souls, in a great measure, depend upon our bodies, and we have great power over our bodies. We can command our outward actions and oblige ourselves to such habits of life as naturally produce habits in the soul. We can mortify our bodies and remove ourselves from objects that inflame our passions. So we have a great power over the inward state of our souls. Again, we can force ourselves to outward acts of reading, praying, singing, and the like. All these bodily actions have an effect upon the soul. As they naturally tend to form such and such tempers in our hearts, so by being masters of these outward, bodily actions, we have great power over the inward state of the heart. So it is owing to this union that we have so much power over ourselves.

Now from this you may also see the necessity and benefit of singing psalms and of all the outward acts of religion. For if the body has so much power over the soul, it is certain that all such bodily actions as affect the soul are of great weight in religion. Not as if there were any true worship or piety in the actions themselves, but because they are proper to raise and support the spirit that is true worship of God.

This doctrine may easily be carried too far. By calling in too many outward means of worship, it may degenerate into superstition. On the other hand, some have fallen into the contrary extreme. For because religion is justly placed in the heart, some have pursued that notion so far as to renounce vocal prayer and other outward acts of worship and have resolved all religion into quietism or mystic intercourse with God in silence.

Now these are two extremes equally prejudicial to true religion. You ought not to say that I encourage quietism by placing religion in the heart. Neither ought you to say that I encourage superstition by showing the benefit of outward acts of worship.

If we would truly prostrate our souls before God, we must accustom our bodies to postures of lowliness. If we desire true favors of devotion, we must make prayer the frequent labor of our lips. If we would banish all pride and passion from our hearts, we must force ourselves to all outward actions of patience and meekness. If we would feel inward motions of joy and delight in God, we must practice all the outward acts of it and make our voices call upon our hearts.

Now, therefore, you may plainly see the reason and necessity of singing psalms. Outward actions are necessary to support inward tempers. Therefore, the outward act of joy is necessary to raise and support the inward joy of the mind.

If any people were to leave off prayer because they seldom find the motions of their hearts answering the words they speak, you would charge them with great absurdity. Now this is very much the case as to singing psalms. People often sing without finding any inward joy suitable to the words they speak. Therefore, they are careless of it or wholly neglect it, not considering that they act as absurdly as one who neglected prayer because his heart was not enough affected with it. For it is certain that this singing is as much the natural means of raising emotions of joy in the mind as prayer is the natural means of raising devotion.

Humility and Pride

From Chapter 16

For prayer at 9:00 a.m., Law suggests humility as the appropriate topic. The example about Caecus (blind), *who is unable to see himself truly, is taken from later in the chapter than the first part of this selection.*

This virtue is so essential to the right state of our souls that there is no pretending to a reasonable or pious life without it. We may as well think to see without eyes or live without breath as to live in the spirit of religion without the spirit of humility.

Although it is the soul and essence of all religious duties, it is, generally speaking, the least understood, the least regarded, the least intended, the least desired and sought after of all other virtues among all sorts of Christians.

No people have more occasion to be afraid of the approaches of pride than those who have made some advances in a pious life. Pride can grow as well upon our virtues as our vices and steal upon us on all occasions.

Every good thought that we have and every good action that we do lays us open to pride and exposes us to the assaults of vanity and self-satisfaction.

It is not only the beauty of our persons, the gifts of fortune, our natural talents, and the distinctions of life, but even our devotions and alms, our fasting and humiliations, expose us to fresh and strong temptations of this evil spirit.

And it is for this reason that I so earnestly advise all devout persons to begin every day in this exercise of humility, so that they may go on in safety under the protection of this good guide and not fall a sacrifice to their own progress in those virtues that are to save humankind from destruction.

Humility does not consist in having a worse opinion of ourselves than we deserve or in abasing ourselves lower than we really are. But as all virtue is founded in truth, so humility is founded in a true and just sense of our weakness, misery, and sin. Those who rightly feel and live in this sense of their condition live in humility.

—

Caecus is a rich man, of good breeding and very fine parts. He is fond of dress and curious about the smallest matters that can add any ornament to his person. He is haughty and imperious to all his inferiors, is very full of everything that he says or does, and never imagines it possible for such a judgment as his to be mistaken. He can bear no contradiction and discovers the weakness of your understanding as soon as you oppose him. He changes everything in his house, his habit, and his equipage as often as anything more elegant comes in his way. Caecus would have been very religious but that he always thought he was so.

There is nothing so odious to Caecus as a proud man. The misfortune is that in this he is so very quick to judge that he discovers in almost everybody some strokes of vanity.

On the other hand, he is exceedingly fond of humble and modest persons. "Humility," says he, "is so amiable a quality that it forces our esteem wherever we meet with it. There is no possibility of despising the meanest person that has it or of esteeming the greatest man that lacks it."

Caecus no more suspects himself to be proud than he suspects his want of sense. And the reason is that he always finds himself so in love with humility and so enraged at pride.

It is very true, Caecus. You speak sincerely when you say you love humility and abhor pride. You are no hypocrite. You speak the true sentiments of your mind. But then take this along with you, Caecus, that you love humility and hate pride only in other people. You never once in your life thought of any other humility or of any other pride than what you have seen in other people.

The case of Caecus is a common case. Many people live in all the instances of pride and indulge every vanity that can enter into their minds and yet never suspect themselves to be governed by pride and vanity because they know how much they dislike proud people and how mightily they are pleased with humility and modesty wherever they find them.

You must therefore act by a quite contrary measure and reckon yourself only so far humble as you impose every instance of humility upon yourself and never call for it in other people. You must be such an enemy to pride that you never spare it in yourself or censure it in other persons.

Now to set out well in the practice of humility, you must take it for granted that you are proud and have been more or less infected with this unreasonable temper all your life.

You should believe also that it is your greatest weakness, that your heart is most subject to it, that it is so constantly stealing upon you that you have reason to watch and suspect its approaches in all your actions.

For this is what most people—especially new beginners in a pious life—may with great truth think of themselves.

If, therefore, you find it disagreeable to your mind to entertain this opinion of yourself and that you cannot put yourself among those who want to be cured of pride, you may be as sure as if an angel from heaven had told you that you have not only much but all your humility to seek.

For you can have no greater sign of a more confirmed pride than when you think that you are humble enough. Those who think they love God enough show themselves to be complete strangers to that holy passion. So those who think they do not have humility enough show that they are not so much beginners in the practice of true humility.

Intercession

From Chapter 21

Law commends universal love as the topic for prayer at noon. This general love becomes specific through intercessory prayer that softens our hearts toward those for whom we pray. The example of Susurrus, the whispering gossip, is taken from the end of the chapter.

A frequent intercession with God, earnestly beseeching God to forgive the sins of all humankind, to bless them with providence, enlighten them with the Spirit, and bring them to everlasting happiness, is the divinest exercise in which the human heart can be engaged.

Be daily, therefore, on your knees, praying for others in such forms and with such length, importunity, and earnestness as you use for yourself. You will find all little, ill-natured passions die away and your heart grow great and generous, delighting in the common happiness of others as you used only to delight in your own.

For those who pray daily to God that all may be happy in heaven take the likeliest way to make themselves wish for and delight in the happiness of all on earth. It is hardly possible for you to beseech and entreat God to make anyone happy in the highest enjoyments of God's glory to all eternity and yet be troubled to see him or her enjoy the much smaller gifts of God in this short and low state of human life.

How strange and unnatural it would be to pray to God to grant health and a longer life to a sick man and at the same time to envy him the poor pleasure of agreeable medicines! Yet this would be no more strange or unnatural than to pray to God that your neighbor may enjoy the highest degrees of God's mercy and favor and yet at the same time envy her the little credit and reputation she has among her fellow creatures.

When you have once accustomed your heart to a serious performance of this holy intercession, you have done a great deal to render it incapable of spite and envy and to make it naturally delight in the happiness of all people.

This is the natural effect of a general intercession for all humankind. But the greatest benefits are then received when it descends to particular instances.

You should always change and alter your intercessions according to what the needs and necessities of your neighbors or friends seem to require, beseeching God to deliver them from such and such particular evils or to grant them this or that particular gift or blessing. Such intercessions, besides the great charity of them, would have a mighty effect upon your heart, disposing you to every other good office and to the exercise of every other virtue toward such persons as have so often a place in your prayers.

This would make it pleasant to you to be courteous, civil, and gracious to all about you, and unable to say or do a rude or hard thing to those for whom you had accustomed yourself to be so kind and compassionate in your prayers.

For there is nothing that makes us love a person so much as praying for him or her. When you can once do this sincerely for anyone, you have fitted your soul for the performance of everything that is kind and civil toward that person. This will fill your heart with a generosity and tenderness that will give you a better and sweeter behavior than anything that is called fine breeding and good manners.

By considering yourself an advocate with God for your neighbors and friends, you would never find it hard to be at peace with them. It would be easy to you to bear with and forgive those for whom you particularly implored divine mercy and forgiveness.

Such prayers among neighbors and friends would unite them to one another in the strongest bonds of love and tenderness. Such prayers would exalt and ennoble their souls and teach them to consider one another in a higher state, as members of a spiritual society, created for the enjoyment of the common blessings of God and fellow heirs of the same future glory.

—

Susurrus is a pious, temperate, good man, remarkable for abundance of excellent qualities. There is no one more constant at worship or whose heart is more affected with it. His charity is so great that he almost starves himself to be able to give greater alms to the poor.

Yet Susurrus had a prodigious failing along with these great virtues: a mighty inclination to hear and discover all the defects and infirmities of all about him. You were welcome to tell him anything of anybody, provided that you did not do it in the style of an enemy. If you would only whisper anything gently, though it were ever so bad in itself, Susurrus was ready to receive it.

When he visits, you generally hear him relating how sorry he is for the defects and failings of such a neighbor. He is always letting you know how tender he is of the reputation of his neighbor, how reluctant to say what he is forced to say, and how gladly he would conceal it if it could be concealed.

Susurrus had such a tender, compassionate manner of relating the most prejudicial things about his neighbor that he even seemed—both to himself and to others—to be exercising Christian charity at the same time that he was indulging a whispering, evil-speaking temper.

Susurrus once whispered to a particular friend in great secrecy something too bad to be spoken of publicly. He ended with saying how glad he was that it had not yet taken wind and that he had some hopes it might not be true, though the suspicions were very strong. His friend made him this reply:

"You say, Susurrus, that you are glad it has not yet taken wind and that you have some hope it may not prove true. Go home, therefore, to your closet and pray to God for this man in such a manner and with such earnestness as you would pray for yourself on a similar occasion.

"Beseech God to interpose in his favor, to save him from false accusers, and to bring all those to shame who wound him by uncharitable whispers and secret stories, like those that stab in the dark. And when you have made this prayer, then you may, if you please, go tell the same secret to some other friend that you have told to me."

Susurrus was exceedingly affected with this rebuke and felt its force upon his conscience in as lively a manner as if he had seen the books opened at the day of judgment.

All other arguments might have been resisted. But it was impossible for Susurrus either to reject or to follow this advice without being equally self-condemned in the highest degree.

From that time to this, he has constantly accustomed himself to this method of intercession. His heart is so entirely changed by it that he can now no more privately whisper anything to the prejudice of another than he can openly pray to God to do people hurt.

Whispering and evil-speaking now hurt his ears like oaths and curses. He has appointed one day in the week to be a day of penance as long as he lives, to humble himself before God in the sorrowful confession of his former guilt.

Resignation to God's Will

From Chapter 22

Resignation or self-abandonment is the topic for prayer at 3:00 p.m.

Whether we consider the infinite goodness of God that cannot choose amiss for us or our own great ignorance of what is most advantageous to us, there can be nothing so reasonable and pious as to have no will but God's and to desire nothing for ourselves in our persons, our state, and condition but what the good providence of God appoints for us.

Further, as the good providence of God introduces us into the world, putting us into such states and conditions of life as are most appropriate to us, so the same unerring wisdom orders all events and changes in the whole course of our lives in such a manner as to render them the fittest means to exercise and improve our virtue.

Nothing hurts us, nothing destroys us, but the ill use of that liberty with which God has entrusted us.

We are as sure that nothing happens to us by chance as that the world itself was not made by chance. We are as certain that all things happen and work together for our good as that God is goodness itself.

This is not cheating or soothing ourselves into any false content or imaginary happiness. It is a satisfaction grounded upon as great a certainty as the being and attributes of God.

For if we are right in believing God to act over us with infinite wisdom and goodness, we cannot carry our notions of conformity and resignation to the divine will too high. Nor can we ever be deceived by thinking best for us what God has brought upon us.

For the providence of God is not more concerned in the government of night and day and the variety of seasons than in the common course of events that seem most to depend upon mere human wills. It is as strictly right to look upon all worldly accidents and changes, all the various turns and alternations in your life, to be as truly the effects of Divine providence as the rising and setting of the sun or the alternations of the seasons of the year. As you are, therefore, always to adore the wisdom of God in the direction of these things, so it is the same reasonable duty always to magnify God as equally director of everything that happens to you in the course of your life.

This holy resignation and conformity of your will to the will of God is so much the true state of piety that I hope you will think it proper to make this hour of prayer a constant season of asking God for so great a gift. By thus constantly praying for it, your heart may be habitually disposed toward it and always in a state of readiness to look at everything as God's and to consider God in everything. Then everything that happens to you may be received in the spirit of piety and made a means of exercising some virtue.

There is nothing that so powerfully governs the heart, that so strongly excites us to wise and reasonable actions, as a true sense of God's presence. But as we cannot see or apprehend the essence of God, so nothing will so constantly keep us under a lively sense of the presence of God as this holy resignation that attributes everything to God and receives everything as from God.

If we could see a miracle from God, how our thoughts would be affected with holy awe and veneration of God's presence! But if we consider everything as God's doing, either by order or by permission, we shall then be affected with common things as they would be who saw a miracle.

For there is nothing to affect you in a miracle except that it is the action of God and tells of God's presence. So when you consider God as acting in all things and all events, then all things will become holy to you, like miracles, and fill you with the same awe-filled sentiments of the divine presence.

Now you must not reserve the exercise of this pious temper to any particular times or occasions or fancy how resigned you will be to God if such and such trials should happen. For this is amusing yourself with the notion or idea of resignation instead of the virtue itself.

Do not therefore please yourself with thinking how piously you would act and submit to God in a plague or famine or persecution. Be intent upon the perfection of the present day. And be assured that the best way to show true zeal is to make little things the occasions of great piety.

Begin therefore in the smallest matters and most ordinary occasions, and accustom your mind to the daily exercise of this pious temper in the lowest occurrences of life. And when a contempt, an affront, a little injury, loss, or disappointment, or the smallest events of every day continually raise your mind to God in proper acts of resignation, then you may justly hope that you shall be numbered among those who are resigned and thankful to God in the greatest trials and afflictions.

Confession

From Chapter 23

Evening prayer at 6 p.m. is a time for confession. As love must be made specific through intercession, so repentance must lead to confession of particular sins through a review of the day's activities. (Note: Law also briefly suggests that prayer before going to sleep be a meditation on the inevitability of death, commending oneself to God's care.)

Evening repentance that brings all the actions of the day to account is not only necessary to wipe off the guilt of sin but is also the most certain way to amend and perfect our lives.

For it is only such a repentance that touches the heart, awakens the conscience, and leaves horror and hatred of sin upon the mind.

For instance, if it should happen that upon any particular evening all that you could charge yourself with should be a hasty, negligent performance of your devotions or too much time spent in an impertinent conversation; if the unreasonableness of these things were fully reflected upon and acknowledged; if you were then to condemn yourself before God for them and implore God's pardon and assisting grace, then what could be so likely a means to prevent your falling into the same faults the next day?

Or if you should fall into them again the next day, yet if they were again brought to the same examination and condemnation in the presence of God, their happening again would be such a proof to you of your own folly and weakness, would cause such pain and remorse in your mind and fill you with such shame and confusion at yourself as would in all probability make you exceedingly desire greater perfection.

Now in the case of repeated sins this would be the certain benefit that we should receive from this examination and confession. The mind would be made humble, full of sorrow and deep compunction, and by degrees, forced into amendment.

A formal, general confession that is considered only as an evening duty, that overlooks the particular mistakes of the day, and is the same whether the day is spent ill or well has little or no effect upon the mind. People may use such a daily confession and still go on sinning and confessing all their lives without any remorse of mind or true desire of amendment.

For if your own particular sins are left out of your confession, your confessing of sin in general has no more effect upon your mind than if you had confessed only that all people in general are sinners. And there is nothing in any confession to show that it is yours unless it is a self-accusation, not of sin in general or such as is common to all others, but of such particular sins as are your own proper shame and reproach.

No other confession but one that discovers and accuses your own particular guilt can be an act of true sorrow or real concern at your condition. And a confession that is without this sorrow and compunction of heart has nothing in it either to atone for past sins or to produce in you any true reformation and amendment of life.

To proceed: in order to make this examination more beneficial, everyone should follow a certain method in it. Every individual has something particular to her or his nature, stronger inclinations to some vices than others, some infirmities that stick closer and are harder to be conquered than others. It is as easy for each of us to know this of ourselves as to know whom we like or dislike. So it is highly necessary that these particularities of our natures and tempers should never escape a severe trial at our evening repentance. I say a severe trial because nothing but a rigorous severity against these natural tempers is sufficient to conquer them.

They are the right eyes that are not to be spared but plucked out and cast from us. For as they are the infirmities of nature, so they have the strength of nature and must be treated with great opposition or they will soon be too strong for us.

He, therefore, who knows himself most of all subject to anger and passion must be very exact and constant in his examination of this temper every evening. He must find out every slip that he has made of that kind whether in thought, word, or action. He must shame and reproach and accuse himself before God for everything that he has said or done in obedience to his passion. He must no more allow himself to forget the examination of this temper than to forget his whole prayers.

Again, if you find that vanity is your prevailing temper, always pushing you to adorn your person and catching after everything that compliments or flatters your abilities, never spare or forget this temper in your evening examination. Confess to God every vanity of thought or word or action that you have been guilty of, and put yourself to all the shame and confusion for it that you can.

In this manner should all people act with regard to the chief frailty to which their nature most inclines them. And though it should not immediately do all that they would wish, yet by a constant practice, it would certainly in a short time produce its desired effect.

Further, as all states and employments of life have their particular dangers and temptations and expose people more to some sins than others, so everyone who wishes to improve should make it a necessary part of this evening examination to consider how he or she has avoided or fallen into such sins as are most common to this state of life.

For as our business and condition of life have great power over us, so nothing but such watchfulness can secure us from those temptations to which they daily expose us.

The poor, from their condition of life, are always in danger of repining and uneasiness. The rich are most exposed to sensuality and indulgence, businesspersons to lying and unreasonable gains, scholars to pride and vanity. So in every state of life we should always in our self-examination have a strict eye upon those faults to which our state of life most of all exposes us.

Again, it is reasonable to suppose that all good people have entered into or at least proposed to themselves some method of holy living and set themselves some such rules to observe as are not common to other people and known only to themselves. So it should be a constant part of their nightly recollection to examine how and in what degree they have observed them and to reproach themselves before God for every neglect of them.

By rules, I here mean such rules as relate to the proper ordering of our time and the business of our common life. Such rules prescribe a certain order to all that we are to do: our business, devotion, self-discipline, readings, retirements, conversation, meals, refreshments, sleep, and the like.

Now as good rules relating to all these things are certain means of great improvement and such as all serious Christians must propose to themselves, so they will hardly ever be observed to any purpose unless they are made the constant subject of our evening examination.

Last, you are not to content yourself with a hasty general review of the day, but you must enter upon it with deliberation.

Begin with the first action of the day, and proceed step by step through every particular matter that you have been concerned in. So you will let no time, place, or action be overlooked.

An examination thus managed will in a little time make you as different from yourself as a wise person is different from an idiot. It will give you such a newness of mind, such a spirit of wisdom and desire of perfection, as you were an entire stranger to before.

Appendix

Reading Spiritual Classics for Personal and Group Formation

Many Christians today are searching for more spiritual depth, for something more than simply being good church members. That quest may send them to the spiritual practices of New Age movements or of Eastern religions such as Zen Buddhism. Christians, though, have their own long spiritual tradition, a tradition rich with wisdom, variety, and depth.

The great spiritual classics testify to that depth. They do not concern themselves with mystical flights for a spiritual elite. Rather, they contain very practical advice and insights that can support and shape the spiritual growth of any Christian. We can all benefit by sitting at the feet of the masters (both male and female) of Christian spirituality.

Reading spiritual classics is different from most of the reading we do. We have learned to read to master a text and extract information from it. We tend to read quickly, to get through a text. And we summarize as we read, seeking the main point. In reading spiritual classics, though, we allow the text to master and form us. Such formative reading goes more slowly, more reflectively, allowing time for God to speak to us through the text. God's word for us may come as easily from a minor point or even an aside as from the major point.

Formative reading requires that you approach the text in humility. Read as a seeker, not an expert. Don't demand that the text meet your expectations for what an "enlightened" author should write. Humility means accepting the author as another imperfect human, a product of his or her own time and situation. Learn to celebrate what is foundational in an author's writing without being overly disturbed by what is peculiar to the author's life and times. Trust the text as a gift from both God and the author, offered to you for your benefit—to help you grow in Christ.

To read formatively, you must also slow down. Feel free to reread a passage that seems to speak specially to you. Stop from time to time to reflect on what you have been reading. Keep a journal for these reflections. Often the act of writing can itself prompt further, deeper reflection. Keep your notebook open and your pencil in hand as you read. You might not get back to that wonderful insight later. Don't worry that you are not getting through an entire passage—or even the first paragraph! Formative reading is about depth rather than breadth, quality rather than quantity. As you read, seek God's direction for your own life. Timeless truths have their place but may not be what is most important for your own formation here and now.

As you read the passage, you might keep some of these questions running through your mind:

- How is what I'm reading true of my own life? Where does it reflect my own *experience*?
- How does this text challenge me? What new *direction* does it offer me?
- What must I change to put what I am reading into practice? How can I *incarnate* it, let this word become flesh in my life?

You might also devote special attention to sections that upset you. What is the source of the disturbance? Do you want to argue theology? Are you turned off by cultural differences? Or have you been skewered by an insight that would turn your life upside down if you took it seriously? Let your journal be a dialogue with the text.

If you find yourself moving from reading the text to chewing over its implications to praying, that's great! Spiritual reading is really the first step in an ancient way of prayer called *lectio divina* or "divine reading." Reading leads naturally into reflection on what you have read (meditation). As you reflect on what the text might mean for your life, you may well want to ask for God's help in living out any new insights or direction you have perceived (prayer). Sometimes such prayer may lead you further into silently abiding in God's presence (contemplation). And, of course, the process is only really completed when it begins to make a difference in the way we live (incarnation).

As good as it is to read spiritual classics in solitude, it is even better to join with others in a small group for mutual formation or "spiritual direction in common." This is *not* the same as a study group that talks about spiritual classics. A group for mutual formation would have similar goals as for an individual's reading: to allow the text to shine its light on the *experiences* of the group members, to suggest new *directions* for their lives and practical ways of *incarnating* these directions. Such a group might agree to focus on one short passage from a classic at each meeting (even if members have read more). Discussion usually goes much deeper if all the members have already read and reflected on the passage before the meeting and bring their journals.

Such groups need to watch for several potential problems. It is easy to go off on a tangent (especially if it takes the focus off the members' own experience and onto generalities). At such times a group leader might bring the group's attention back to the text: "What does our author say about that?" Or, "How do we experience that in our own lives?" When a group member shares a problem, others may be tempted to try to "fix" it. This is much less helpful than sharing similar experiences and how they were handled (for good or ill). "Sharing" someone else's problems (whether that person is in or out of the group) should be strongly discouraged.

One person could be designated as leader, to be responsible for opening and closing prayers; to be the first to share or respond to the text; and to keep notes during the discussion to highlight recurring themes, challenges, directives, or practical steps. These responsibilities could also be shared among several members of the group or rotated.

For further information about formative reading of spiritual classics, try *A Practical Guide to Spiritual Reading* by Susan Annette Muto. *Shaped by the Word: The Power of Scripture in Spiritual Formation* by M. Robert Mulholland Jr. covers formative reading of the Bible. *Good Things Happen: Experiencing Community in Small Groups* by Dick Westley is an excellent resource on forming small groups of all kinds.